Results Generate Results

*Sports Data & Agility,
Tennis and Pickleball*

Results Generate Results

Sports Data & Agility,
Tennis and Pickleball

Jhonnatan Medina Alvarez
Laura F. Poe, Ph.D.

Additional contributions:
Graphic Design Illustrations by Jennifer Dioguardi
Edited by Piper Phillips

<u>Triumph</u>

For those who think they can't.
For those who become overwhelmed.
For those who fear trying.
For those who focus on failure.
Know this.
Failure does not exist.
With every attempt, you learn.
With every learning, you grow.
With growth comes progress.
Progress leads to opportunity.
Opportunity leads to triumph.
You are amazing!
It's time to show the world.

-Laura F. Poe

DEDICATION & ACKNOWLEDGEMENTS

To my parents, Maria de la Paz Alvarez, and Carlos Medina, for always giving me their 100% unconditional love and dedication throughout my tennis profession and life. To my best friend and confidant, Maria Lopez, for her unrelenting friendship and always answering the phone to talk when I needed someone during our three decades in the world of tennis. To my professor and mentor, Dr. Laura Poe, for giving me the push to use my knowledge for the greater good. To coaches Kathy Riley and Kayla Miller for their love and care during my stages of self-discovery. And to all my coaches and players during my 30 years in the sport of tennis. I can only say that this book contains a little piece of each one of you.

I would like to give credit to my beloved sister Jennifer Dioguardi for designing the cover that represents the combination of tennis and technology. I would, also, like to thank those who took the time to read this book and help us through the editing process.

To my beautiful wife, Piper, for your never-ending love and support. You helped me focus and finish this lifetime project. Finally, to my son, Leonardo Vicente, you are the anchor that brings calm to my soul.

Gracias,
Jhonnatan Medina Alvarez

Aunque mal Paguen Charles…

RESULTS GENERATE RESULTS

A MESSAGE FROM THE AUTHORS

Jhonnatan Medina Alvarez

Tennis is an extremely personal and emotional sport that deals with a constant search for opportunities to create winners, force errors, and most importantly adapt to the different rhythms of the match. Most of us understand the complexity as we mature within the sport and through our experiences every time we step on a tennis court. For me, after 30 years of exposure to a variety of levels of tennis, as well as numerous coaching environments in the domestic and international competition arenas, I realized that the amount of data tennis players must store to gain a great level of mental skill could be overwhelming. These skills are defined as problem-solving, adaptation, analysis, shot selection, accuracy, control, self-discipline, and awareness.

These skills can be hard to master if you are not exposed to a deeper process of understanding them. Hitting the tennis ball for many players, including myself, has become second nature. Therefore, after discovering a new world of information systems and cyber security, I learned that tennis lacks a solidified process to comprehend data that identifies all the necessary components to create a mental report both during matches and between each point.

This insight that I gained from my tennis career as a Division 1 Head College Coach, and my academic pursuits as a university student, allowed me to validate and successfully test most of the things that I did not understand during my playing years. Now, I want you to learn as I did how to collect, process, develop, and distribute data. That knowledge will unlock a perspective that will make a world of difference in the right understanding of the sports of tennis and pickleball. Concepts such as vulnerabilities, requirements, and acceptance will become your foundation to create and advance your game along the way.

In this book, I will fuse all the knowledge that I gathered during my tennis, coach, and scrum master careers, and

share the unique approach that we call *Sports Data &
Agility (SDA)*. This sports-based methodology will
provide a better understanding of tennis holistically,
instead of just a hitting and playing not to lose concept. I
want you to start moving away from those boring lessons
and the endless mindset of "I don't know what's going
on," or "I don't see myself getting better," to a more
detail-oriented understanding of the protocols and
procedures required to be present during all stages of
learning. You will develop internal leadership, deactivate
negative patterns, and gain access to your unlimited tennis
or pickleball potential.

In 2022, I was searching for a way to continue my passion
for sports, and I was introduced to pickleball, the fastest
growing sport in America. I had the opportunity to apply
the SDA methodology, described in this book, when I
decided to begin my pickleball journey. I had no
knowledge of this sport when I began, and within six
months, I was playing the top players in the world.
Applying this methodology allowed me to learn the sport,
evaluate my progress using the data, and create a specific

training program to develop the required skills needed to be successful in my new passion of the pickleball sport and my overall goal to become the best player that I can be.

Jhonnatan Medina Alvarez

Laura F. Poe, Ph.D.

I've been in the business world for roughly 25 years, and nearly all of those years have been working on some type of system implementation project. Through my experiences with many different technologies, companies, and teams, with members of varying backgrounds and cultures, one thing remained constant – the teams were always focused on a specific goal within a finite period. In business, project managers and Agile team coaches provided direction and a framework for the teams to perform the work. As the Agile methodology swept through corporations, becoming the modern practice for rapid delivery, people realized they could apply this methodology for home projects and generic activities. After all, managing a technical project, a construction project, or a home project is not so different when stripped of their technical area of expertise.

In 2020 and during my role as a professor of Information Systems and Cyber Security, I had a student in my class whose background could not have been further from the field in which he was studying. That student was Jhonnatan Medina Alvarez, a former professional tennis player. During one of our first conversations that led to many more, I listened to him talk about his role as the Director of Tennis as he looked for avenues to redirect his career into business. I started seeing similarities in the way he coached his teams and the way I coached project teams in the business. I realized there was an opportunity to create a methodology that could be used in sports to help both teams and individuals achieve higher levels of performance and do so faster. Most of the time, coaches are doing their best to help players improve but do not have a systematic approach and do not have quantitative forms of measuring progress. This challenge was something Jhonnatan and I decided that, collectively, we could solve. His experience in sports and my experience in business could be leveraged to allow sports coaches, managers, and players to achieve their highest results. After all, creating successful habits will result in success.

Combining our expertise, we created the *Sports Data & Agility (SDA)* methodology. We tested this methodology with beginner players in the early stages of training in tennis and pickleball. Applying SDA resulted in increased player performance, and the players were motivated when provided with quantitative measures of their progress on a daily, weekly, and cyclical basis. Not only were they motivated, but they were accountable for their progress. Our handbook provides specific approaches using SDA that any coach or player can apply to achieve success.

Laura F. Poe, Ph.D.

Contents

Perform – Ready to Play?
- Ego Shots
- Shot Tolerance
- Tournament Performance

Review – Results
- Self-Assessment
- Results Review

SDA Progress Board

Real Life Application – Game On!
- **Example: Maria Alvarez**
- **Conclusion**

Templates

Biography of Jhonnatan Medina Alvarez

Biography of Laura Poe

QUOTES

This book contains inspirational quotes that we hope will challenge you to persevere.

"FREEDOM IS NOT POSSIBLE WITHOUT CARE. IT IS THE NATURAL CONDITION OF OUR EXISTENCE TO COMPREHEND THAT WE NEED A CONNECTION NOT ONLY TO OURSELVES BUT MORE IMPORTANTLY TO OTHERS." - JHONNATAN MEDINA ALVAREZ

INTRODUCTION

Throughout history, sports have allowed individuals, groups, and nations to compete using a combination of physical and mental skills. People, by nature, thrive on competition and challenges. Competition begins early, whether for attention, to be first in the lunch line, score the first soccer goal, hit the first home run, or win the first match. Competition is emotional. No one wants to lose, and we learn through many experiences how to best manage our emotions. Independent sports, such as tennis and pickleball, are fully accountable to the player. During individual matches, there are no team members who contribute to a loss or a win. There is only the player. Becoming the best player takes dedication and planning. Yes, planning! Like any goal in life, there must be a plan to achieve.

In business, speed is one of the key factors of success in the marketplace. Consumers want to buy the next greatest product, and whoever releases it first has the edge over competitors. This is true for all consumer-based products. For years, companies generated plans marching towards a specific go-live date, with everyone crunching to meet the date, working extra hours, and often sacrificing quality. The Agile methodology provided an entirely different approach for the business world, one where companies no longer focused on a single date to finish developing their product. Instead, they focused on making small, incremental improvements that could be applied and released to the market much earlier than waiting until the final product was complete.

In sports, the player often has a goal to be the best, or to compete in a specific tournament, but progress is usually made in small, incremental steps. At first, the player is a beginner, with no knowledge of the sport. Over time, the player improves, but the improvement does not always have quantifiable measurements. In Olympic sports, each competitor is judged on specific aspects for computing a final score. This data gives the player something to use to measure progress. Not all sports have technique and form measurements applied to their plays. There is either a winner or a loser. Improving performance requires knowledge of one's progress as well as a means to evaluate and adapt to an opponent. Sports Data & Agility methodology was developed by combining many concepts used in business product development to the industry of sports. This book discusses the application of Sports Data & Agility to the tennis and pickleball sports and includes specific terminology related to these sports throughout each chapter. Jhonnatan Medina Alvarez provides numerous stories relaying his experiences in coaching and playing professionally.

What is SDA?

We have created the *Sports Data & Agility* methodology for players to plan and track progress on goals they establish. Like the popular Agile framework that guides the journey of product development, sports require the same adaptations to increase skill levels over time. Sports require continuous improvement and development, with a focus on precision to succeed. Coaches bear the responsibility of being both observers and approvers of the final product, the player. They help to define goals in partnership with the player, or perhaps the player's parents when younger children are learning a skill. Additionally, coaches provide the training needed to refine and develop skills. Their roles are critical to the success of the player, but the player must have the motivation to succeed. Otherwise, the coach's efforts will not be realized. Players must put in the time and be committed to succeeding. Just like learning a new skill in a job, practice is essential.

We standardized this methodology into a repeatable process that can be used for every skill and every level. The Sports Data & Agility (SDA) methodology provides a framework that both coaches and players can follow to set goals and track progress over time. All too often, coaches guide players, but there are no measurement tools or standard processes that document the steps the players must follow to improve, or how to measure progress and test skills. SDA can be applied to individuals as well as teams by adapting the goals, measurements, and testing of progress.

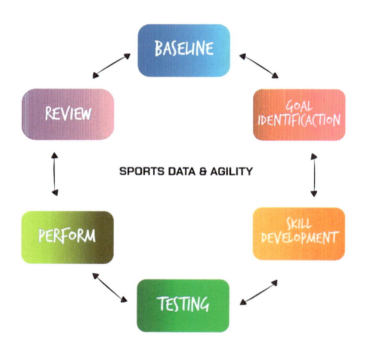

For SDA to be successful, there must be trust between the coach and player while empowering the player to own their progress. SDA offers flexibility for every player at every level. The progress can be quantifiably measured and tracked with visible results and gives transparency to the player, coach, and team. One of the greater benefits of SDA is its ability to apply it to a single player or an entire team. Tennis and pickleball are sports of individual and dual modalities, for that a coach is focused on both the individual and the team.

Tracking everyone's individual progress while simultaneously tracking a team is a daunting task when there is no standard means to document each player's skill levels. This causes coaches to guide the team with a generalist approach. Coaches give every player similar guidance to help the entire team, and there is less time for focus on the individual player. Players spend hours practicing, and the key feedback is their performance in the next match. How did they do? Did the player win or lose? The important question is not whether the match was won or lost, but why. The answer depends on which specific skills were being developed through the personalized goals and plans.

As a coach, after working with so many players, it became evident that a form of measuring and documenting the progress was needed. This is a two-part system. First, a process for identifying their current level, setting goals, and tracking them is needed. Second, measurement of their progress in individual lessons based upon their consistent and accurate strokes and responses to plays provides meaningful input on how they are performing and where the weaker areas lie.

SDA's framework is based on the player's ability to plan and gives the coach insight to best direct the player to improve. For a team, this leads to better overall group performance and higher rankings. For the player, this results in higher rankings, higher level tournaments, and eventually sponsorships or scholarships based on the player's overall performance. The time put into the planning will yield results on the court.

SDA follows the player from their starting point to the end of their goal and is divided into six different phases: **Baseline, Goal Identification, Skill Development, Testing, Perform, and Review**. Each of these phases is explained in this book with examples for coaches and players to follow for generating and tracking their own individual plans. The SDA process flow shows the progression through each phase of the cycle. Flexibility to change the approach or refine a goal is critical. Because each player's individual capabilities are so different from another player's, skill development might not occur as quickly as planned for the cycle. The objectives for the player may need to be adapted, even mid-way through the cycle, to accommodate the player's personal abilities. For this reason, the arrows are in both directions, indicating the ability for a player to go back and modify their objectives and tasks.

How to Achieve the Best Results

The Sports Data & Agility methodology operates on an iterative basis, using a period agreed upon by the coach, the player, and the player's support system. The support system encompasses the group of individuals who provide the player with the support needed to be successful and is often family members, such as parents, siblings, or close friends. The support system is important to include in decisions affecting the player, as they are often responsible for financing the player's lessons, taking a young player to and from practices, and providing for other needs as they arise.

Before beginning, you must determine the length of time you want to plan, develop, practice, and test your goals. We call the length of time a cycle, and it encompasses an entire rotation of SDA. Typically, cycles are three weeks long to progress through each stage of the process and produce a final measurement of progress. If preferred, they can be two weeks or even four weeks. The key is to set a consistent cycle and one that allows for true skill progression. Three weeks is used throughout this book, because it represents a cycle that provides sufficient time for players to improve and allows for a match at the end of the cycle. Once the process ends, it will repeat itself by establishing a new baseline, training, and performing with different goals in each cycle.

In tennis or pickleball, the final goal may be to compete in an international or national tournament and achieve the highest ranking or rating possible. For a novice player, many skills need to be developed to achieve the level required for competing. Players must continuously improve the basic strokes and movement, learn the strategies of the sport, and develop an accuracy and consistency level that is sufficient for a beginner to enter a tournament. The accuracy will continue to improve with a focus on the different goals, objectives, and tasks.

"ONLY YOU HAVE THE POWER TO SHAPE YOURSELF." - JHONNATAN MEDINA ALVAREZ

BASELINE

Identify your starting point

Software development is an activity-based upon constant change to remain competitive. The technology teams support the business and are critical to its success in a consumer-driven market that wants everything faster and better. Translating this same premise to sports means players can respond quickly to feedback, track what they changed, and document the results of how each change impacted their competition. It requires knowing your competition.

Before developing a plan, ownership must be defined. Is it the player or the coach who owns the progress? Ownership depends on the stakeholder. Coaches of a team might say they own the plan. A personal trainer might say the player owns the plan. With an individual sport, such as tennis or pickleball, if the player does not take accountability for the plan, then skill development will fail. To improve, the player must be dedicated to the plan.

In Sports Data & Agility methodology, the initial step is to establish the player's **baseline**. The baseline is determined through a series of measurements of basic skills required for the sport. *This baseline should represent the current skill level.* In tennis and pickleball, this may be the number of times a player can hit the target using a forehand, backhand, or a volley, to name a few strokes. Multiple measurements will likely factor into the consistency and accuracy rating to determine the player's areas of strength and the skills that need additional practice. Establishing the baseline is critical for measuring success and must be an honest, data-driven assessment of the player's skill. Without an accurate baseline, the player cannot measure progress or establish goals, and the final performance will be affected.

Important Considerations

1. The baseline will change every cycle.
2. The baseline must be a true representation of the current skill level.
3. The baseline must be measurable.

Jhonnatan

> I remember many times during my tennis and early academic career that my mind would always play tricks on me by not allowing me to differentiate

among growth, learning, and/or winning. I wish someone had been able to explain to me when I was younger what I have learned after years of emotional distress. There is a way to evaluate oneself with great understanding and without having to get caught up in feelings and emotions, as many of my players, friends and even professional colleagues will express after a negative outcome in a match. Given these experiences, I am confident that my journey traveling the world for 15 years playing tennis and now as a professional pickleball player has given me the ability and tools to help anyone to be the best version of themselves.

My main quest is to bring light and awareness to all stages of learning in the sport of tennis and pickleball, and most importantly, to provide a methodology that will allow you to avoid losing more time or having members of your family looking for the special ingredient to help you become a successful player. The reality is that with hard work, dedication, self-motivation, and discipline, you will be able to prepare yourself to perform and endure all the challenges and adaptations that you will need to have to move up in the amazing sports of tennis and pickleball. Let's start by understanding the meaning of identity, and for that, we will be using tennis and pickleball vocabulary terms throughout the course of this book to get more connected to our unique perspective of the sports.

What happens when during a tennis match, we finish our last point of the set, and it is time to have a 120 -second break and change sides on the court? Or during a pickleball game when we have a maximum of two minutes before starting a new game? Usually, during the changeover, we drink water and use our towel to dry off sweat, most of us are trying to figure out what is happening in the match or game, what needs to be done to maintain a favorable score or upgrade the strategy to get back in it!

Those internal conversations are necessary to mentally self-organize and create a work in progress (WIP) mentality. That is what *identify your starting point* means in tennis or pickleball terms. Now, we need to dig deeper and create a mental database of our experiences. What is a mental database? To respond simply, it is all the memories that we have gathered throughout the trajectory of our tennis and pickleball lives that are being stored in our minds from day one.

Jhonnatan

> When I shared this personal concept, it took me back years and reminded me of how my parents used to always tell me to keep myself focused and out of trouble as I was a hyperactive kid. They would say, "Your brain is a computer; go back and evaluate what you've learned from that experience." However, this never resonated with me during my younger years. I never understood why it was of extreme importance to have a clear evaluation of the conditions that we are subjected to during every game/match, training,

or even life. The opponent's vulnerabilities need to be exploited to gain an advantage. Without this, understanding your ability to create the right process would be hard to implement.

As we establish a baseline, we will find opportunities to think logically rather than emotionally, helping us to determine how to create patterns and validate them based on our strategy. The result will be improved overall performance. For example, let's think about this scenario. You are playing a powerful player that has an aggressive forehand and is making you respond without any time to think, just pure reaction. At that time, the thought is typically, I can't beat this player. If you have data about the opponent's vulnerabilities and can apply that data on the court, then you will be able to purposefully respond. There is always a starting point for every player. You just need to understand that if you change the shot selection (height, spin, and placement), the ball's power will decrease or even become easier to defend, opening new opportunities to achieve the point and control the tempo of the match. *"Remember to get something you never thought was possible, you must do something you have never done." - JM*

When identifying vulnerabilities, strengths, and the different strategies and environments, it is important to keep in mind that these adjustments will help us to create a profile of the adversary and pinpoint the location of our data to reproduce a well-developed plan, and for that, we will need to talk about self-awareness.

Self-Awareness

Most of us have our interpretation of what *self-awareness* can do for or against us during an emotional decision. Self-awareness is an ability to understand emotions at a higher level by creating a better picture of the best course of action, without losing perspective of our performance. This was a struggle for Jhonnatan during his career because of how much it meant for him to win at all costs. The lack of self-awareness hindered his ability to respond to change, and in tennis, this is key to being adaptable to your circumstances, especially in situations in which you need to play a different tennis style. This awareness for most players takes us out of our comfort zone, something that we try to avoid for fear of the unknown. Every decision will lead to more data we can gather about our current skills.

The next time you step on a court, you need to perform a self-assessment. Play to get better, and you will see the results when the work has been done correctly. Consistency will yield results. During Jhonnatan's early years when he was diagnosed with ADHD (Attention-Deficit/Hyperactivity Disorder) and regularly struggled with hyperactivity and impulsiveness. He found that thinking and understanding his purpose before acting became better than any pill that he could ever take. Self-awareness is critical to improvement.

What every coach, mentor, or parent wants for their player or child is to play joyfully and with self-control. Remember that performing at a great level for a long time requires constant self-awareness and reflection, because in every competition, you will face challenges that you must be able to recognize, observe, and readjust yourself accordingly. To achieve this, you need to train and build situations during practice that will help to improve your decision-making and increase the level of tolerance you have for stressful situations.

Know Your Why

Another aspect that we call knowing *your why* is extremely important in understanding what motivates you to succeed. What is your motivation for tennis or pickleball; how far do you want to go in your quest for success? During self-awareness, we expose some of the importance of why we need to be aware of the impact of our choices. It is important to keep a smooth transition throughout the course of tennis or pickleball training and matches. We need to be precise in navigating the various reasons that each decision will bring. Where is it coming from? How do the impediments to your success attempt to break your mental strength? Make sure your strategy wins the battle over negativity as the match evolves.

As players, we lack detailed knowledge of identifying *your why*. Sadly, in our opinion, the tennis and pickleball industries need to continue investing in mental and emotional growth, which is vital to the development of a player at any level. More frequently in tennis, we see overrating technique, perfectionism, and use of overpower as the most effective solutions. For that, Jhonnatan would like to use himself as an example with this personal perspective.

Jhonnatan

> During a dark part of my career, I became injured by using a low tension in my racket. This made the shape of my forehand and backhand stroke overcompensate with the use of my wrist in point of contact and follow through, making my left thumb hyperflex. This ultimately made the tendon weak and caused my finger to slip away from my hand. Even though this injury still allowed me to play through high amounts of pain and numerous movement restrictions, the emotional toll was increasing daily. Since my pain would not subside,

my mind began to look for a way to gain an opportunity at all costs.

Having all these barriers, I was firmly committed to pursuing my dream. I started to have a conversation with myself, as I call it, 'go for a walk', and tried to unlock new ways to play to stay competitive in my career. One day during my internal conversation in a practice, I realized that everything we do when we play can be reused for future experiences to get the next point, and so on. Keeping track of everything became my focus. I slowly became more aware of my opponents' point construction, patterns, and emotional impulses upon specific balls and strokes on the court.

Realizing the importance of gathering specific data on myself and my opponents became a motivation. I started collecting raw data. It took me a long time to determine the type and level of data and create a pathway to achieve *your why*. When I was placed into a position that had no exit, my mind created an alternative, rooted in the necessity of accomplishment. This showed that we all can rise above and persevere, but you need to be hungry for success and self-respect. At this point, everything started to take form for me, which all started from the struggle.

Look at the most successful people in the world. They all came from a place where they struggled, a time when they needed to understand the noise, and ultimately, they needed to adjust their strategy. There is no self-development without struggling and overcoming challenges. My experience enabled me to identify and comprehend the data gathered for any player, and my decision-making was based upon my opponent's vulnerabilities instead of a monologue of all the reasons why it was not working out. The success of my strategies was already implied in the score. There was no need to overthink the things that were not working for me. I needed clarity and direction. Remember the main reason your tennis or pickleball competition is negatively affected is from not being able to evaluate the opponent's strokes, patterns, and game plan.

During my college coaching career and later in my pickleball journey, I took *your why* to a new level. The importance of systematic information became more obvious. Collecting and reviewing data is necessary to become more flexible and adaptable.

Like the Agile project methodology, SDA is based on transparency, a high level of commitment, and adaptation. Through Jhonnatan's experiences, it became his mission to apply that methodology to sports. SDA requires continuous self-assessment to progress, develop, and become a more all-around player and athlete.

Part of establishing a baseline is to understand your current overall capabilities. To determine a baseline, your current level must be determined through a variety of tests that can help track, compare, and re-evaluate a player's progress, and then this data can be applied during planning to establish goals. This same template can be used repeatedly for establishing a new baseline for every cycle and again for planning.

Tennis and pickleball are complex sports that require high levels of fitness, technique and strategy. Tennis matches may go on for hours, and the player must have adequate stamina. Conditioning and endurance should be part of the regular fitness routine as well for technique upgrade and maintenance. To support good results during daily training, players must eat properly with limited sugars and added proteins. Most importantly, water intake is necessary to prevent dehydration during every cycle of training and competition.

Jhonnatan

When I was finalizing my last year in the 14 and under division in 1996, and during my training travels, I was sent to train at a prestigious academy in Florida for a few months. At my arrival, the lead coach shared with me, after many technical tests that covered my grips, swing shape, mobility, and control upon different ball speeds, that I needed to change my forehand grip and take-back. At that exact time, I was jumping into an all-new tennis division with players almost fully developed physically and technically. Despite this, I was one of the best-ranked players in my country of Venezuela, as well as internationally. My support system advised me that regardless of my current success, the results of my technical skills test demonstrated significant areas for improvement. If these areas went unaddressed, they would negatively affect my transition into the new age division.

Looking back years later, I am grateful for those findings at the right time, and even though it took me time to upgrade my grip and take-back, the results, in the end, were extremely positive. My ranking not only went up nationally in the new division, but I was able to be Top 30 in the world as a junior player. Remember, the baseline is your safe house, the place you go to check your overall progress and identify where you currently are to be able to set future performance goals.

"EXPLORE YOUR DEEPEST THOUGHTS AND BECOME WHAT YOU DREAM OF EVERY DAY WITHOUT BEING AFRAID OF THE CHANGE." - JHONNATAN MEDINA ALVAREZ

GOAL IDENTIFICATION

Time to Plan

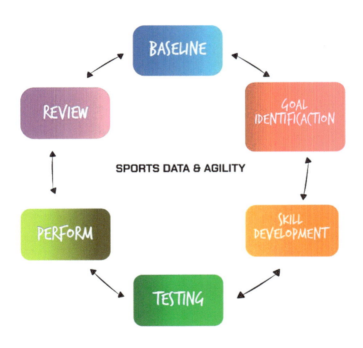

No one goes from beginner to expert in a single season. In **Goal Identification** the key at this stage is to identify one or two areas of improvement and focus on developing these specific skills for a three-week cycle.

Long-term goals should be identified at the beginning of the season. Given there are four seasons in a year, we plan on a quarterly basis. This gives us 12 weeks for a long-term plan, divided into four cycles, three-weeks per cycle. If a player's long-term goal is to place in the top 10 for the season, then all the short-term goals should support the long-term goal. This phase of SDA is the most critical because the coach should develop goals for the season as well as goals for each cycle for a given player. The more work that is put into planning, the more significant the results will be, provided the player puts forth the effort and follows the tasks identified in the plan.

Each tennis or pickleball season should be broken into four cycles of three-week time increments. At the beginning of the season, the coach determines the goal for the player (or team). Understand that if this goal is dependent upon winning throughout the four cycles, the overall goal would constantly change based upon game/match wins, and losses. Therefore, the goal itself should remain the same throughout all four cycles regardless of this. The goal may be to participate in a championship tournament, but the player (or team) does not have enough wins to make it to the tournament. Rather than changing the goal, the best practice would be to focus each cycle on gaining more skills to support the player's progress to winning more matches. In the end, the goal of participating in the championship tournament may not have been successful, but there were many successes identified throughout the season.

Another way to identify the season goal is to focus the goal on the player's skills rather than just wins and losses. A beginner may not have an opportunity to compete in a tournament, because the skill level is beginning at ground zero. Therefore, the season goal could simply be to have enough skill level to compete in several matches. Goals can be more or less aggressive based upon the player's desire to compete. For instance, the beginner may want to compete in a certain number of matches and have a minimum percentage of wins.

Pack Your Bag

Jhonnatan

> There is not a day that I don't find myself going over experiences and memories from my playing or coaching tennis career since I started playing

pickleball. *Packing your bag* by far was something that I will always treasure with all my heart. The main reason is that it was my alone time with the components that were essential to my preparation and performance. I find it hard these days when I see players that are extremely unprepared to train or compete. Planning is essential to gaining access to the right data to know how we can improve and evolve throughout our careers.

I remember when my parents saw my tennis potential at the beginning of my career. They struggled to find the right fit for me when it came to coaching, facility, and environment. For many years, we found ourselves compromising our own life and schedules to meet the needs of the coach's availability and/or finding open courts to be able to train.

These negative obstacles reinforced the need to create a solid training system and support team during my quest to have a set yearly plan.

Additionally, I realized that I needed to develop a mentality of self-trust in many areas of my tennis, including technical, cognitive, physical, social, and tactical development. The outcome of this adaptation had many advantages, such as becoming extremely self-motivated and disciplined. However, on the other hand, my overall tennis knowledge in many cases was not accurate and needed real direction and specific mentoring.

Thankfully, through receiving many years of quality instruction, formal education, and leading others as the Director of Tennis in different facilities, I was able to design specific plans to accommodate players on a daily, weekly, monthly and yearly basis. For the players I coached, custom training plans were created, complete with different phases and long-term development goals to have an entire year of data. Consequentially, tennis players under my leadership consistently developed more in accordance with their chronological age, ranking, and expectations. The customized training plan allowed me to be flexible with the amount of time I, as a coach, needed to spend in the different areas of their overall tennis competition.

The importance of planning cannot be underestimated. The components need to be based on the current needs of the player, especially in the developmental and competitive stages. Those can be measured by level, physical ability, and most importantly, dreams (the player's goals). At the same time, it is important to recognize the value of a player's support team. Without a strong support team, a player will struggle during the different phases that are required to create a sustainable and measurable performance plan.

Having the details of the player's skill level in every category is essential. Without these details, we are unable to achieve the competitive goals and are training without purpose. Therefore, it is necessary to start your plan with measurable training and tournament goals while always focusing on the end goal.

Pack your bag is not just a towel and a shirt being stored in your tennis or pickleball bag. Packing your bag is about being proactive in gathering all the data necessary to be successful at the short-term, interim, and long-term goals. Goals should always be set by the player with the consent of the support team, as they all should have to share the progress with different levels of importance. For example, when Jhonnatan's professional tennis support team met for a planning meeting, they decided to play in Brazil for five weeks.

Jhonnatan

> We began the process of self-awareness immediately by questioning the environment that I was going to be subjected to with questions, such as: How high we are from sea level? What surface and type of ball is the tournament using? What is the weather like this time of the year? What is the cut-off of the main draw? Will I play the qualifier

round if I do not get in the main draw by ranking? All these questions were fundamental in creating a mental map to visualize changes in the daily and weekly plans that were going to be required before traveling. The goal was to gain 10 Association of Tennis Professionals (ATP) points by the end of five tournaments.

The planning started with three weeks of basic preparation and one week of specific pre-competition. Training matches were added to ensure all the previous processes that were developed from the preparation plan could be tested and added to the pre-competition stage that required working on strategy and game patterns. What was the outcome of this specific planning? One of the best tours I ever had! Over the five weeks that I played, I was able to not only achieve the main goal of 10 ATP points but surpass it with 28 ATP points awarded to my singles ranking. Also, my second goal to create a positive winning/losing ratio was achieved. The message is clear for this chapter, developing a plan is everything, and we need to be specific in all the layers of growth that are important for improvement. The planning process is essential to the understanding of your game or match, your vulnerabilities, and your strengths. These items should show, in detail, how your data will dictate the steps of refinement and specific design of your game.

To put it into practice using our framework, the goals and their corresponding objectives must follow the SMART guidelines:

- **Specific** (small and reasonable)
- **Measurable** (able to be evaluated quantitatively)
- **Achievable** (can be accomplished within a cycle)
- **Realistic** (within the player's skill level)
- **Timely** (established with target dates)

Similar to the life cycle of a business project that uses the Waterfall or Agile methodology, goals will translate into requirements. To satisfy the end goal for the player, the requirements must be met. Writing the goals is one of the most critical aspects of SDA.

"MAYBE IT'S JUST ABOUT BEING WILLING TO OPEN UP TO YOURSELF, HOLD AN INTIMATE CONVERSATION AND BECOME VULNERABLE IN ORDER TO GROW."
- JHONNATAN MEDINA ALVAREZ

SKILL DEVELOPMENT

The Aces

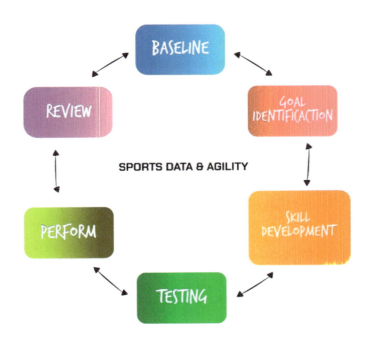

During **Skill Development**, the focus shifts from documenting the goals and objectives to the action of performing each of the tasks. The coach leads the player through the proper exercises and measures the daily progress. Much like with software delivery, the coach is reviewing each stroke and gives corrective guidance. The greatest benefit here is the documentation and measurement of the progress.

In software development, impediments may arise that prevent the team from delivering a functional product. These impediments can be outside of the control of the team. In sports, however, few scenarios prevent an individual player from completing their goal. Impediments could be injuries, scheduling conflicts that limit practice time, or lack of coaching knowledge. Coaches, players, and the support system must work through solutions that will allow them to continue to progress and meet the objectives within the cycle. Progress requires daily modifications and measurements.

Skill development is divided into *The Aces*, which stand for Adaptation, Agility, and Accountability. Each of these deliver's value to your overall growth.

Adaptation

For most tennis and pickleball players, adaptations are the changes that represent what players are required to perform, both inside and outside of the court.

Jhonnatan

One of the most profound words that I ever heard was adaptation. Throughout my years of playing and coaching tennis and now pickleball, that word continues to be my beacon. Adaptation represents the constant development of hard and soft skills. The sport itself is unpredictable. Players must understand and embrace a process that will require them to be adaptable. Playing good tennis or pickleball will not guarantee that you will win, and many times, we do not feel on top of our game which is the real challenge. The word *timing* is often used to explain the feeling when we hit a ball. Timing will vary due to our interpretation, but I still found that regardless of the feeling, our main goal is to win. Adapting your ability to be resilient to environmental factors, your opponents and your ego is essential.

After this explanation, the right question is, how can we better adapt during the match? The answer is simple. You need to be willing to surrender to your own ego. Many times, I was exposed to scenarios that required a high level of adaptability. For example, I was playing with a specific type of racket for the first two years of my professional career, however my ranking was not improving. During four-week tour in the Middle East back in 2001, my coach at the time was always looking for opportunities to increase my level of tennis. One night after a long match, my coach advised me that my racket was not providing the defense and acceleration needed during point construction. This meant that my ball was not creating enough acceleration to fulfill my playing style, and I was not able to defend properly on the run.

These issues let my body feel extremely tired because I was compensating for my racquet's lack of response, causing me to exert more strength. It was taking me longer to recover between matches, especially my dominant hand (lefty player). Even though my coach's perception was accurate, I felt that a racket could not possibly have that much impact on my overall game. However, I agreed to use a new racket to play the following matches, with the condition that I would be using the same string, grip, and tension. The new racket had all the characteristics that he thought would allow me to save energy, defend better, and create more opportunities with a heavier ball and more acceleration. At this point, you are thinking, did he say next match? Yes, you read it right. Not the next tournament, but the following match, which was in two days! Talk about making adaptations; I was thousands of miles from home, forced to adapt to my environment while making changes to my game without having my support system present for encouragement.

We decided the tournament goal would be to gain experience and the ability to overcome change rather than focusing just on winning. Since I did not have much time to adapt to the new racket.

It was a hot day around 1 pm in Saudi Arabia. I was playing the second round against the number one player from Portugal, who was a great player with an amazing backhand. The conditions on the hard court were difficult, and the balls were heavy. During the entire match, I proposed to only focus my mind on thinking about my opponent's vulnerabilities. I figured out that he wanted me to make a forced error with my backhand or provide an easy shot for him to win the point (create a winner). As a personal goal, I decided to let the racket show the data, and regardless of any mistake, remind me to be mindful of the progress that I would gain from this experience. During the match, I noticed the racket enhanced my lefty abilities making me more productive in a variety of shots.

The most important information gathered after winning the match, was that I had gained more power and control, significantly improving my defense with less effort and pain. Specifically, the data indicated I was able to create at least 20% more breakpoint opportunities and had fewer unforced errors.

Using the new racket for the remainder of the tour of Middle East, I gathered the same number of points that I previously earned with my old racket over the course of a year. The verdict? Adaptation is invaluable. Work on it because it pays off when you least expect it.

Let's talk about how we can master this *ace*. SDA is a process that provides you with a way to record your goals and measure your results. The first thing we need to understand is that SDA allows flexibility and adjustment to issues or a new set of outcomes that requires new approaches in order to achieve the goal. We need to be more knowledgeable in all the areas of our competition to continuously upgrade our tasks during training and matches. If our process, decision-making, and flexibility are slow, our competition will suffer in many areas that are critical to a positive outcome in our planning.

Agility

Agility is necessary to become flexible to changes that you will experience whether on the court or in your environment. Agility is not just an action but is a state of being.

Jhonnatan

> Let's take an experience from my coaching background to show a better picture of what SDA can do for you and your tennis or pickleball.

> During the beginning of my coaching career at the collegiate level, I had several players that required a higher level of understanding and versatility. However, my first thought was to increase intense

training as a normal requirement for improving their tennis skills. As time went by, I realized that I needed a different approach. That's when I decided to invest in my self-organizing and cross-functional skills to understand each player's needs and wants. Months later, the results were tremendous. Not only was I able to get more versatility from each player, but at the same time, they became more open to adaptation as obstacles appeared.

The process became quicker and easier to resolve, and that alone created a higher level of self-awareness. They felt empowered to see options and new venues to succeed. Their success could be tied directly to the new set of protocols and procedures. The players felt safer and more secure. They were walking the path without fear. Consequently, they understood that versatility was part of being an agile player. Do not forget what we discussed about creating a mindset of continuous development and improvement. We need to leverage the data we gather about our performance to respond to change with great flexibility.

Accountability

To advance, we must be *accountable* for our own development, successes, and setbacks, which requires self-reflection and action. Accountability is an area where we can constantly improve. Making excuses is easy, but taking accountability requires us to take ownership of our plan and how we performed.

Jhonnatan

I found during my years of coaching and playing that having the ability to accept and take complete ownership for your decisions leads to success. For tennis and pickleball players, we have the tendency to be focused on ourselves as individual performers and not take time to acknowledge how our choices can impact our support system. I admit to making many selfish decisions during my career due to egocentric behavior and being spoiled by having early success. Now, looking back, I reflect on the importance of accepting my flaws, committing to change, and trusting the process. Be aware of your surroundings when you make decisions that do not conform to someone, such as an opponent, referee, or anyone close to you. Have courage to say, I am sorry. The world needs more servant leaders. I guarantee your tennis/pickleball and personal life will thank you later.

Skills are not developed overnight. Once we have our baseline from the first phase of SDA and we have established our goals, we can practice our skills throughout the three-week cycle. By the end of the cycle, we should have measurable improvement that can be seen in the data we have collected in our consistency and accuracy. During the review phase, we come back to the baseline and determine the progress. However, it is at this phase where that skill development occurs. This is a period of constant practicing and performing the tasks identified.

The lesson plan developed during **Goal Identification** is executed daily throughout the cycle. While the work of setting up the goals and tasks may seem arduous initially, the data can provide more meaningful observations. Coaches and players can review how they progressed and where more self-correction is needed.

Regardless of the stroke, the player's placement of the ball must be tracked and measured. With each rally, where is the player's ball landing? Is it landing near the service line, baseline, or mid-court? Is the player pushing the ball to fulfill the task? If the player is unable to meet the task of 10 rally balls by placing the ball on the court without going out or hitting the net, then the player cannot continue to the next task. Skill development occurs after identifying any issues you are encountering with technique. Developing consistency is more than just completing the planned 10 rallies. Not only do we need to understand if the player is consistent in their delivery of the stroke, but can they place the ball on the court with accuracy? You can be consistently accurate or consistently inaccurate. The biggest challenge is the process of becoming consistently accurate.

Lesson plans are created to support the tasks and ensure the player achieves each individual task. While goals themselves may go beyond a cycle, the objectives and tasks should be completed at the end of every cycle to get closer to completion of the goals we set.

"ULTIMATELY, IT IS A CHOICE BETWEEN WHAT YOU WANT AND WHAT YOU NEED. BE HONEST. YOUR INNER SELF IS ALWAYS LISTENING."
– JHONNATAN MEDINA ALVAREZ

TESTING

Competition

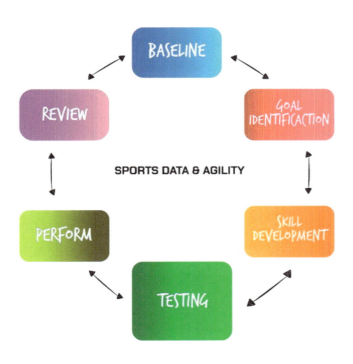

Testing a player's progress against their objectives is achieved through a training or *competition* match. During the match, there should be noticeable improvement in the player's skill (technical, physical, tactical, and emotional) level. Remember that the improvement should be directly tied to the overall goals set forth during this cycle. The player should be evaluated in terms of the future (long-term) with respect to their cognitive and emotional growth.

One of the important aspects of testing in tennis and pickleball is that it allows us to understand the continuous assessment process that is happening in our competition, whether it happens during the development of our strategy, shot selection, technique, and even in our critical thinking. In many cases, we disregard the element of failure and do not use that data as a form to connect with our IQ growth. In Information Technology (IT), testing is one of the most important steps to complete a project.

This detailed examination allows the developer to know if everything is completed after evaluation, and from there, it will be ruled as completed and ready for production. Thereafter, all those protocols ensure the authentication of withstanding different environments successfully for a later user-friendly experience. If we take this IT explanation of testing and compare it to the majority of players' mentalities, the tendency is to attach testing with failure. This is because when we take a shot and we miss it, our mind goes to automatically to negativity, self-doubt, and most importantly lack of accountability. A player could avoid taking ownership and blame the racket or paddle, but it never improves the outcome of the competition. We need to keep an open mind and let the data tell the story. Without testing shots, patterns, and behaviors, we will only be hitting a ball without a purpose.

How can we embrace this new idea of making a mistake with a smile? If we understand the purpose of the competitions of tennis and pickleball, then testing things out will become the most powerful resource to always have. We test everything that we do. It is a normal and interesting behavior of the human condition.

Back to our main concept, we need to test, collect, and retest. First, we need to know that as explained in the previous chapter, there is no wrong answer, just another opportunity to learn from the experience. Second, if we are not able to see it, then it becomes obvious that we are not aware of these important items, and we need to train accordingly. This is a priority as you are making decisions on every ball, and those must be explored to later as the match progresses.

Jhonnatan

> During my years as an owner and Director of Tennis at MetroWest Tennis Academy, I constantly dealt with the pressure from parents, players, and even myself to bring real feedback to every lesson and avoid vague summaries of their progress in areas, such as control, accuracy, and tennis IQ. I developed a set of tests that would bring real data to a training session. Interestingly,

even before getting my degree from Longwood University, I was playing with data.

This methodology from the SDA is designed specifically for tennis and pickleball but can be adapted to any other sport and even real-life events, such as school or any other activity that requires a sustainable process in place. Now, let's go back to the importance of testing. This initiative will allow any player to know who they are in terms of something I call, *What's Your Number?*

7 3 12 5 8

What's Your Number?

This concept means that every player will repeat a specific stroke during each point for a specific number of times, usually until they fail, break, or miss. During the early stages of developing technique and movement, tennis and pickleball players will make mistakes that will increase the unforced error ratio. This gives many free points to the adversary and makes the likelihood of winning extremely low.

As you go over all these testing scenarios, you will end up with a good amount of data that will make it easier for the player to know how much training is required in areas of control or accuracy depending on the stroke.

Jhonnatan

> After my injury, I became afraid to take shots that could hurt me again, and from that perspective, I started making sure that my process and selections were accurate based on what was going on during the match. For example, if I was 40/0 serving instead of going for power, I would try to create a fast-paced slice body serve and take the net so that I would keep the offensive position. At the same time, I was working on other game styles and pattern changes needed to keep the player guessing.

As a strong reminder, let's reinforce that testing our shot selection will be based on our behavioral pattern during each point, analyzing whether you are putting all your daily training and sacrifice into a low percentage, emotional shot. If you are using emotional shots, you will most likely not succeed in the overall goal to win the match. Your results will be temporary. Play with a purpose and walk away from relying on emotional shots. In reality, no one cares if you make a twiner, as there is no award for that in this sport. Be responsible and accountable by defining purpose and self-control. It's your choice, and for that, there is no one to blame but you, so respect yourself!

The Rule of 3

Many times, during the service game, one can easily lose track of the data, such as not tracking where to place the serve, know the stroke needed from the type of spin added to create a return, and finally, taking over the position to attack the next ball. *The Rule of 3* focuses on first creating a plan from the beginning of the point, starting from the serve (first shot) to bring the right weight, speed, and placement. Then, the second shot, (return from the opponent) will most likely come back defensively, as a slow-paced ball allowing for a better opportunity to take over the point construction and make the point (third shot). At the same time, if the starting serve is weak, slow, and without placement, then the return will be strong with precision and aggressiveness, making the third shot a defensive one.

The idea is simple: during your service game, it is key to select each serve with the understanding of the score and the previous reactions from the opponent. Knowing in detail what type of serve the opponent likes and dislikes, a profile can be created, stabilizing a better range of serve. *The Rule of 3* is about maintaining the offensive position as a server by respecting the other player's virtues and vulnerabilities along the game to minimize breakpoint opportunities and pressure upon second serve moments.

"YOU MUST RESPECT YOUR OWN PROCESS. BE STRONG AND STAY CONSISTENT DURING THE DIFFERENT LAYERS OF GROWTH. DON'T BE AFRAID. REMEMBER YOU HAVE YOURSELF TO GUIDE YOU EVERY STEP OF THE WAY." - JHONNATAN MEDINA ALVAREZ

PERFORM

Ready to Play?

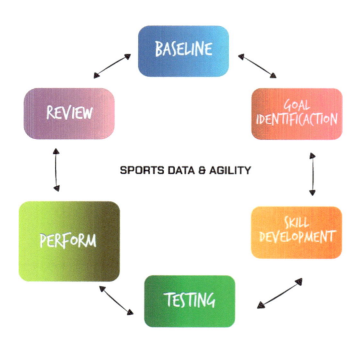

In business, there is always a demo of the final product. The stakeholders need to see evidence of the work that was performed, and this final product review should meet the original expectations, which we call requirements. The same review is done in sports, but usually, it's in the form of a competition, such as a match. The match/game is the final accomplishment, allowing the player to demonstrate the skills learned during this cycle. **Perform** is a final assessment of the player's skills. Going back to our goal planning, the perform phase represents the official tournament. Perform is the curtain call, the game, the match, the recital, etc. This is where the player pulls everything together.

Daily Training → Practice Match → Official Tournament

Creative adaptation in a process can occur with a positive outcome. We need to have resilience despite the outcome and keep moving forward. Our outlook must be in line with our choices while knowing that action will bring a reaction. When performance happens on the court, we can enjoy the struggle of a beautiful competition. The concept is quite simple. To perform, we must evolve constantly during every shot and decision made by both us and our adversaries. Perform is a word that can lead to many places in our understanding of the unique journey of tennis and pickleball.

Jhonnatan

I remember walking by the tennis courts of the Venezuelan Tennis Federation after a match and other players would ask me, "Hey, Medina, did you win?" and I would reply "Yeah, I won!" with all the ego in the world. Unfortunately, the reality was that even after winning the match, what was the level of performance? Did I play from the ego? Or did I commit to the stipulations of my support team and planning? Most of the time during my junior years, I struggled to understand the goal of performing. If I could go back in time, I would explain a couple of things to spare myself the trauma of losing matches that still haunt me.

In my last years of college coaching, I needed to show my players that great performance is a choice regardless of any impediment that might come our way. There are many measurement scales for the requirements to perform in the workforce, sport, and arts. To me, it is necessary to systematically review what it will take to achieve personal or group satisfaction.

Let's take the example of theater. I had the privilege to understand this creative and inspiring world in detail during my last class in college. In theater, everything is done with the mindset that the show must go on regardless of any impediment. Actors, directors, and everybody else involved in the production of a play needs to have a high level of commitment to the greater good of the experience. Even if they are struggling during an act, everyone is dedicated to improvisation, allowing the performance to continue. If we apply that to tennis and pickleball, we need to recognize our impediments and be ready to evolve.

Ego Shots

Ego shots are the dream shots that will give us famous but unreliable status in the tennis or pickleball community. Our necessity to try these once in a lifetime shot is just part of our human condition. However, it can be detrimental to the overall goal of creating a consistent and disciplined mindset that is fundamental to being competitive every time we step on a court.

During our lifetime, we identify behaviors relative to our position. Each moment brings a decision, and there is nothing more valuable than the score. The reason is that it dictates what we are playing for during that specific moment in the match. Only time gives players the experience to fully understand the situation. How many times did you ever lose a match or game by playing the important points poorly? Are you tired of saying, "I was winning and then I lost?" To be consistent, you have to rely on the data and not use ego shots which are emotional and can derail your overall strategy.

Jhonnatan

> As the competition progresses to the final points, you should understand that the choices you are making will start to have a bigger impact on the outcome of the competition. When you are playing to win, you need to be more aware of decisions, patterns, and patience during each situation. A lot of players have a fear mindset and say to themselves, what happens if I miss? When you are playing not to lose, you become too caught up in the outcome of the match without being present, leading to more errors.

Shot Tolerance or Play by the Number

Winners occur when the opponent is unable to touch the ball and are often the most influential shots in tennis and pickleball. Unfortunately, winners require a high level of accuracy that in moments of pressure are extremely difficult. Anyone can make a winner, but not everyone can store the data and average number of strokes being hit and missed at a specific time. A pattern should start to emerge between players.

During points, players will give you an estimate of how many shots it takes until their technique breaks down during each stroke. *Shot tolerance* is one of the most productive strategies to use against your opponent. The goal is to break down their strokes by focusing on their ability to continuously hit them until they miss. The way to do this is to create different patterns based on speed, height, and spin that ultimately will increase the probability of an error. In important points, the average of unforced errors will rise during high stress moments, providing a picture of the strategy that should continue to be implemented, meaning that if the player misses their backhand every 5 balls, you should continue to play at that specific number or higher.

Therefore, the team or player must be trained to control their emotions and to recall the number of shot repetitions that end up in error. This information should always be applied during the competition. Players with a good ability to handle pressure will use the data to be patient, explore the opponent's strategy, and create a pattern to break any stroke.

Tournament Performance

Demonstrating skill improvement from all the work previously learned is the main intent rather than simply focusing on the outcome of the competition. It's easy to get caught up on winning and losing. If we win, we can label our progress as successful, but the review allows us to reflect on more than just a winning or losing. Everyone should understand that performing is a key step to determine how much improvement was achieved in the overall competition, particularly in how stressful situations during a tournament were handled. The performance will demonstrate how the player adapts to the overall environment, opponent, and expectations.

"SEE THE BEAUTY IN THE STRUGGLE. IT IS ALL A LEARNING EXPERIENCE. ALL THAT YOU NEED IS IN YOUR SOUL. OPEN YOUR HEART TO WHAT IS MEANT FOR YOU." - JHONNATAN MEDINA ALVAREZ

REVIEW

Results

The **Review** phase of the SDA methodology is our point of reflection. We have worked hard to achieve the goals and finished our performance, but how did we do? What did we do well or not so well? What should we continue doing or stop doing? What new skills or training methods should be employed? In business, following a large effort, we perform *lessons learned* to evaluate what kinds of things we may want to do differently to be more successful. Lessons learned can, also, focus on team cohesion and interactions with stakeholders.

Once again, sports require that same reflection to improve. After a baseball game, coaches pull the team together and discuss things they could have done differently, such as fielding the ball between the bases to get a double play. They may review their batting line-up to put stronger batters at the front in hopes of getting on the scoreboard at the beginning of the game. Future practices may be adapted to reinforce the areas where the team was weaker.

Tennis and pickleball players should review their competition to see when they lost key points, where they won important points, and why. Areas of weakness translate into future goals. Regardless of the sport, time is spent reviewing the performance. The player's performance, regardless of winning or losing, still requires evaluation.

Self-Assessment

Without exploration, there is no purpose of discovery for growth or information. The aftermath holds the most important part of enlightenment for anyone that is looking to learn from experiences. *Self-Assessment* means having the courage to be reflective and accountable to your support team for your match performance and why you won or lost. It's of extreme importance to dissect every detail for valuable information, perform an assessment on what occurred during the past working cycle, and identify actions for improvement going forward. If we understand that process and we transfer it into our planning conversations, it will lead to what we did well and what we can improve, instead of avoiding any type of gathering of information for fear of being exposed to failure.

Players, coaches, and family members often avoid the self-assessment, which can lead to negative communication and animosity between everyone involved. Improving processes is important and can be achieved by evaluating all the items that players and support teams gather during a specific match or training session. Proactively having those conversions helps drive the goals that the player and support team agree on during planning.

Knowledge on the court is measured by our capability to know how to overcome a game plan by a specific player. Sometimes we think that is about us, and if we play our game, things will come into place, and we will secure the win. When we cannot realize that our game plan should be based on the perspective of adaptability and flexibility, we will enter a part of the sport that is chaotic and lonely.

This negative loading is based on a constant mindset of being rigid and negative.

Jhonnatan

> I can share many examples during my career about struggling with being in a negative loading state for entire matches at a time. It took me a while until I was able to eliminate that mindset and start readjusting my mind and strategy. Unfortunately, it was often too late during the match, and I still suffered an unfavorable outcome.

> Given the losses that I experienced for years, it was high time to make a change. I realized that growth occurs when we struggle. When we are comfortable, complacency follows, and we don't seek to change or improve. We stop evaluating ourselves and begin placing blame on those around us without reflecting on how our own actions and attitude impact our performance. We need to have great self-awareness and take accountability for the consequences of our

actions, modify our strategy, and be open to adapting in order to grow.

In Agile, Scrum Masters are similar to sports coaches, and one of the important parts of the job is to provide encouragement and direction for improvement. As teams build products, they are, also, building their process. Team members can review and explore how to become more efficient and productive. It is of extreme importance to learn how to have a *inspect and adapt* mentality, which is something derived from business that can be directly applied in sports. In tennis or pickleball, to win a tournament, you need to beat six players if you are playing a 64-player draw. As much as you are an amazing hitter, many components are going to play an important role in winning repeatedly.

Results Review

Competition provides test performance and demonstrates that the player has met the objectives. The test is not a pass or fail based upon a win or lose, but it's a method to demonstrate the specific skills, whether it was improving a serve or a backhand, during a match or game.

The *Match/Game Review Form* is a simple template for anyone to use to provide players with clarification in their process. There is nothing more important than sharing a couple of minutes right after training or competition and having a well-defined acknowledgment of the outcome of the performance. The use of video recording can be extremely important to recount important moments during the competition and have detailed data to view with your support system during your post-competition meeting. I guarantee that after that review of the process with yourself or your support system, things will become clearer and easier to navigate. Collecting this data during competitions is critical for planning, monitoring, and demonstrating progress.

MATCH/GAME REVIEW FORM

Name: **Date:**

Dominant Hand:

Opponent Name:

Surface:

Weather Conditions:

QUESTIONS	ANSWERS
What did you do well in today's match/game?	
What could you have done better in today's match/game?	
What did the opponent do well?	
What did the opponent not do well?	
What can I adapt to my process to improve after today's match/game?	

CONCLUSIONS:

SDA PROGRESS BOARD

As the work progresses, we can track the progress on a visual board that allows the player and coach to show advancement against each objective. The progress board is managed over the cycle time described in **Goal Identification**. We are using a three-week cycle time, because three weeks allows the player to work towards skill development that can be applied to playing in upcoming matches. However, this cycle can be adapted to two-weeks or even four, depending upon the established goals and what the player wants to accomplish. However, the recommendation is to start with three.

The objectives are tracked daily to determine the progress made for each one. Tracking can be done for each supporting task if the player or coach desires a more detailed level of daily progress. All goals actively being pursued are listed on the overall board for visibility and to remind the player of their vision. The goals shown should only be those for the current cycle. There should not be any objectives without the corresponding supporting goals. Every objective should be completed during a cycle, which means that every supporting task must, also, be completed.

The SDA board is comprised of five different statuses to track progress. These can be tracked using existing tools that are used to track business projects, such as GitHub or JIRA, or manually using post-it notes or a whiteboard. We can define each status as follows:

To Do: The objective has not been started.

In Progress: The objective has begun; the player is working on the tasks and following the lesson plan.

Test: The objectives are ready to be tested in a match and remain in this status until the match has been completed.

Review: The matches have been completed, and they are being evaluated to determine if they passed the test and can be considered complete

Complete: The objective was accomplished.

Not all objectives will begin at the same time, so there may be objectives in the To Do column mid-way through the cycle. This example board shows how the objectives move across the board during the three-week cycle. At the end of the cycle, all objectives should be in Complete status. A good check for the coach is the ensure that all objectives are at least in progress mid-way through the cycle, otherwise the player's ability to accomplish it diminishes.

"I KNOW YOU CAN.
BE STRONG." - JHONNATAN
MEDINA ALVAREZ

REAL LIFE EXAMPLE

Game On!

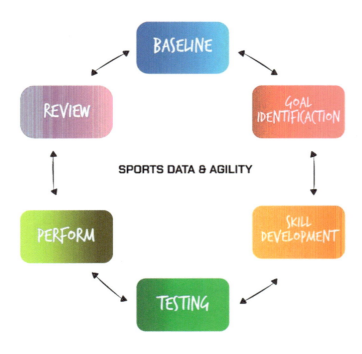

To put SDA into context, let's use an example of an actual player, who we will call Maria Alvarez. As we go through each phase of SDA, we will track Maria's progress from her baseline to final review. Maria's example will apply to both tennis and pickleball. Her overall plan must be well-written and agreed upon by her coach (Jhonnatan) and support system (parents/friends).

Let's start with the **Baseline**. In this stage on the SDA Maria will be given different tests to know her current tactical, technical, physical, emotional, and competitive status. For this example, we will provide a *Fitness Test Form* and *Technique Testing Form* for Maria to explore her current physical and technical levels. These items will share a precise evaluation all her overall abilities. We will use that data to establish the next phase of SDA.

FITNESS TEST FORM

Name: Maria Alvarez

Date: 1/1/22

Age: 18

Weight: 130

Height: 5'8

TEST	INSTRUCTIONS*	TEST 1	TEST 2	TEST 3
1. Hexagon				
2. Medicine Ball Throw				
3. Spider Drill				
4. Side Shuffle				
5. 30 feet (10 yard) Dash				
6. Side to Side				
7. 1.5 Mile Run				
8. 1 Min Push-Ups				
9. Plank by Time				
10. 1 Min Pull-Ups				

* Look online to find intructions for each fitness test

TECHNIQUE TESTING FORM

Name: M. Alvarez	GRIPS					
Age: 18	FORE	BACK H	VOLLEY F	VOLLEY B	SLICE	SERVE
D Hand: R	✓	✓	✓	✓	✓	✓
Backhand: Two						
Notes:						

MOVEMENTS

CLOSE	OPEN	SEMI – OPEN	SLIDE	RECOVERY STEP
✓	✓	✓	✗	✗

STROKES

PREPARATION				POINT OF CONTACT				FOLLOW THRU			
F	B	V	S	F	B	V	S	F	B	V	S
✗	✓	✓	✓	✓	✓	✗	✗	✗	✓	✗	✓

SERVE

SLICE			FLAT			SPIN		
PREP	POINT	FOLLOW	PREP	POINT	FOLLOW	PREP	POINT	FOLLOW
✓	✓	✗	✓	✓	✓	✓	✗	✗

After the baseline is recognized, Maria and her support system will move into **Goal Identification** to review the data and set up short-, medium-, and long-term goals based on the five categories that we previously mentioned. It is important to be specific and realistic when setting up the goals during the planning session. Once her goals are established, objectives are created that will support each goal. Each objective must, also, meet the SMART guidelines. Most importantly, the goal must be attainable and individualized. Tennis and pickleball require adaptation and problem solving. For players struggling with strategy identification, a customized plan should be created for improving tactical knowledge. Maria's first goal based on priority will be to learn how to identify her opponent's strategy.

Tactical Goal: Using data gathered during an official game/match, successfully identify opponent's strategy, and implement new tactics as needed.

Objective 1: Learn how to identify strategies from different opponents after retrieving the data from training points played.

- <u>Task 1:</u> Assess opponent's vulnerabilities and patterns.
- <u>Task 2:</u> Add different patterns (offensive and defensive) to identify vulnerabilities and strengths.
- <u>Task 3:</u> For each vulnerability, repeat or change the pattern process and gather data.
- <u>Task 4:</u> During an important point, acknowledge the opponent's vulnerabilities, how the opponent reacts, and make modifications as necessary.

Understanding how we measure completion is critical to be able to assess if she met her objectives and overall goals. We create a definition of complete to establish criteria for this assessment.

Definition of Complete: Maria was able to successfully identify, collect, and store the opponent's data to recognize patterns, determine a game plan, and establish a shot selection. Maria needs to be able to create her profile and introduce a set of tactics to avoid exposing her vulnerabilities. The goal was to maximize every opportunity to win points on the court, which will lead to success.

Each objective must be achievable during the cycle. Goals that cannot be completed within the three-week cycle should be broken down into smaller, more achievable goals. As Maria's coach I should see performance improvements each day. If her goals are not measurable, then I will be unable to track the progress. Another important aspect of goal setting is to establish goals beyond your three-week cycle.

CATEGORICAL GOAL PLANNING

Name: Maria Alvarez Date: 1/1/22 Age: 18 Dominant Hand: R	**Short Term Goals**	**Medium Term Goals**	**Long Term Goals**
Tactical	Identify opponent's strategy, implement new tactics	Open the court with short angles	Change the pace of the match at any time
Technical	Improve shape of the shot on the forehand	Adapt stroke preparation to different court surfaces	Achieve self-correction in a live environment
Physical	Learn how to run diagonally	Increase muscle mass	Perform at the physical level of an athlete
Emotional	Don't play not to lose (play to learn)	Don't have a negative self talk on court	Control your body language
Competitive	Play two tournaments every month	Top 20 in Virginia	Compete in a national tournament

Based on the objectives above, we have created a training plan that would allow Maria to achieve each task, thereby completing the objectives, and ultimately achieve the goal. At the end of each cycle, I will measure Maria's progress against the goals. The *Weekly Training Cycle Form* below provides a specific training regimen that aligns with the categorical goals.

Now we will design a set of tasks and share in detail Maria's *Weekly Training Cycle Form*, which starts her **Skill Development**. We will begin working on delivering daily value to everything that Maria and the support system committed to. Training will be key and of extreme importance to increase the level of control, accuracy, and confidence, since the goal is to create strategies for high pressure situations. Please remember that if there are limitations or vulnerabilities in your weekly or daily training, a new course of action should be created to close that gap.

WEEKLY TRAINING CYCLE FORM

CONSISTENCY

MONDAY

warm up 10 cones serve
150 Ball middle
150 Cross each side
150 Down each side
150 Slices
Total 600

SKILL SHOTS

TUESDAY

warm up
30 Min hand feeding
Accuracy drill 4x4 square
cc/cl/dp

DEFENSE & OFFENSE

WEDNESDAY

warm up
50 Ball control high pace
50 Ball slice vs slice
50 Ball slice vs spin
50 Ball mix
50 Square controls

ADAPTATION

THURSDAY

warm up
100 Ball control
1,2,3,4,5, Lap X control
10 Ball progression (back)cc/cl/dp
3 Ball progression (back)

STRATEGY / PLAY

FRIDAY

warm up
10 Min open play
10 Min specific defense scenarios
10 Min play by the number
10 Min specific defense scenarios
30 Min match/game

TOURNAMENT / RECOVERY

SATURDAY

Tournament

Add goals to the following
Technical
Tactical
Emotional

TOURNAMENT / RECOVERY

SUNDAY

Tournament
After the completion of the tournament fill out the match/game review form

As we feel empowered by the data collected it is time to move into a key part of the SDA methodology, known as **Testing.** We will use the *Daily Lesson Plan* to specify our daily work within each week cycle.

The plan was to guide Maria through an open-environment training where she can freely make her own decisions while playing points for 10 minutes with each player. At this time, the goal was for her to work on finding the game style of her opponent and adapting her game to overcome them.

Maria's warm-up focused on improving hand-eye coordination by catching balls with her dominant hand while moving in the direction of the ball. After the warm-up, we reviewed how important the lesson's goal was to prioritize decision-making and adaptation.

In the first 10 minutes, Maria played against a counter-puncher player, which she described as a someone with great footwork and consistent strokes. She told me that this caused her to adapt her game to be more aggressive and take over the net in a timely manner, resulting in winning most of the points.

In the second 10 minutes, she played a net player. She had a hard time with this game style. She told me that the player had great serves and would always come to the net every chance she had. In the end, Maria reflected on her performance, saying that she did not find a way to neutralize it, therefore, lost many points.

In the final 10 minutes, she played against a lefty player. Maria happened to find this player's game style to be one of her favorites because of how much versatility the player had. The player challenged her to play many different types of shots, but she was able to win the majority of points by using the information she had on her opponent and adapting her response to their shots.

Cool Down:
Maria did a group jog and socialized with the other players while stretching afterwards.

Coach Evaluation:

One of the greatest gifts of coaching is when a coach can work alongside a player and see in real-time how they respond to different strokes and situations. For Maria, introducing a new understanding of the game by showing her the different playing styles was extremely important for her overall tactical goal. She was able to provide great feedback about her performance and accept healthy criticism. The transfer of knowledge must be accepted by the player for them to actionably improve future performances.

Coach Conclusion:

Maria had to overcome different patterns and mental obstacles. She had to show progress on how she was able to view the vulnerabilities of the opponent for each point played, won, or lost. After reviewing her performance data, Maria had to review her accuracy during each play and create future strategies to gain the advantage over her opponent. Her ability to inspect and adapt her thought process required understanding the environment to which

she was exposed. In this lesson with Maria, her attitude
and passion for learning was outstanding.

DAILY LESSON PLAN FORM

Monday

Player: Maria Alvarez
Date: 1/1/22
Coach: Jhonnatan Medina Alvarez
Time Frame: 1 hour
Objective: Tactical
Cycle: 1 (3 weeks)

BREAKDOWN	TIME
Warm-up: Dynamic warm-up	**10 minutes**
Lesson detail: Working on understanding the different game styles and how to adapt to them Warm up (hitting) 10 minute points with three different players	**30 minutes**
Cool Down: Light jog plus a stretching	**10 minutes**
Evaluation: Introducing a new understanding of the game by showing the different styles was extremely important for her overall goal	**5 minutes conversation during cool down**
Self-awareness: Improved the ability to overcome different patterns and mental obstacles.	**5 minutes conversation during cool down**

At this point, Maria's SDA work is almost complete. After completing testing, Maria needs to move into the **Perform** phase by competing. This will determine if the skills she developed during training show enough progress towards her goals and meet her definition of complete.

In the beginning of the competition, Maria was too intimidated and hesitant after recognizing the opponent's weakness to implement her tactics. However, she was amenable to identifying the weaknesses of her opponent and adapting her technique for hopeful success. Remember, regardless of the outcome she will have learned a lesson and grown.

Thankfully, Maria was able to beat her opponent in the match and move to the next round. Afterwards she cooled down with a light jog and some stretching. Meanwhile we documented her feedback about the style of her opponent and identified how she responded to such style.

By the end of the tournament Maria was successful regardless of the outcome because she met her tactical goal by successfully increasing her ability to inspect and adapt based on the opponent's strategy and subsequently adjusting her game style. Another important part of her performance was that she was able to beat a player that in the past she never did, this showed growth on her part and that our planning produced results. Finally, she was able to gather useful data for our final review.

Recording competitions is an important tool to use to provide transparency. This gives visual support to use with her coach and allows her to see important aspects that will be used in our last phase of the SDA review. Specifically, her behavior, strategy, movement, technique, and key moments in the match. All these items shown visibly will help her continue to upgrade her ability to analyze any opponent.

After all the phases in the SDA methodology we can move into the last part, **Review**. I asked Maria to fill out the *Match/Game Review Form* as seen below to record data gathered from the competition, including her reactions to her opponent, specifically, responses to patterns, decision making, and vulnerabilities. These results were evaluated against her tactical goal to determine if her performance passed her objective. For sharing purposes if she did not pass her objective, then she must go back and rework that skill.

After the review was completed, Maria established new criteria for identifying other players' game plans and patterns. For the next cycle, she can create new objectives using this data.

MATCH/GAME REVIEW FORM

Name: Maria Alvarez   **Date:** 1/1/22

Dominant Hand: Right

Opponent Name: Stella Sobreira

Surface: Hard

Weather Conditions: Indoors

QUESTIONS	ANSWERS
What did you do well in today's match/game?	My decision making was really good
What could you have done better in today's match/game?	Slow down during the game, especially when I am losing
What did the opponent do well?	Does not overhit and played consistently during the entire game
What did the opponent not do well?	Dinks cross court more often than not, becomes somewhat predictable
What can I adapt to my process to improve after today's match/game?	Incorporate calmness and intention in every shot selection

CONCLUSIONS: I need to play at a slower pace overall. When I am doing well and in control, playing fast can play into my favor, but when I lose control, playing fast compounds the issue and makes me drop my level very low.

To provide a visual, here is an example of a progress board following Maria through one cycle. One dependency on the support system is noted here. In this case, the player does not have transportation and is dependent on the support system to ensure that she can make it to practices and individual training time as needed. The cycle is identified as three-weeks in duration, and this is the first cycle being tracked for Maria.

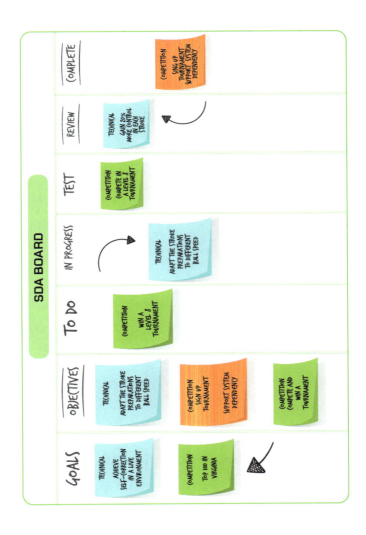

CONCLUSION

Using the SDA provides a framework for achieving a goal using timeboxed plans and measurable criteria. Regardless of your goal in life, whether it is achieving a degree or certification, become the best sports player, track projects, or even work towards a desired fitness level, creating a detailed plan is the first step in achieving that goal. If the planning stops there, then as soon as we encounter obstacles, we will be unable to overcome them. Our obstacles can be external or even internal, and we must reflect upon our own commitment to progress. The benefits of SDA are numerous: a defined process; tracking mechanisms; templates for your use; and most of all, a framework that can be repeated an endless number of times.

We started out by identifying your baseline, which served as your starting point. Every time you repeat the SDA process, you establish a new baseline. Using the baseline, you identified goals, objectives, and tasks, and you determined how you would test each of them in matches or games. You created daily lesson plans that supported each of the tasks. These daily lessons can be modified every cycle as your goals change. You will be able to reflect upon previous baselines and see your own progress after every cycle. Seeing that progress can generate a feeling of accomplishment.

Your competition performance served as a test against your tasks. The outcome of the performance was not specifically whether you won or lost the match. The focus remained on the specific skill development you were targeting in your goal and plan. Evaluating the opponent's vulnerabilities in addition to your own vulnerabilities were recorded as valuable data. You may repeat competitions and daily lessons until you have an acceptable result in your progress. This testing and skill development can be repeated until you have met your objectives and are ready for your final performance.

The final performance is the go-live, the curtain call, the tournament where all the goals should be met. Again, the overall goal in sports is always to win, but the tournament performance should be evaluated against your specific goals. You could win the match but fail to meet your overall goals in improving a stroke. Reflecting on our performance requires self-discipline and a mindset open to critique. Using the data from your final performance will serve as input into your next cycle plan.

While this book focused on tennis and pickleball, the SDA process can be applied to any sport. We hope that you will be able to leverage the framework and apply it, whether for you as an individual or as a team coach. You can even coach yourself using SDA and establish habits that will make you successful. SDA is more than just a framework. It is a template for success.

For questions or to hire Jhonnatan Medina Alvarez for personal coaching services, please visit his website at http://www.thejmax.com.

"HABITS ARE CREATED BY REPEATED ACTIONS THAT EVENTUALLY BECOME UNCONSCIOUS BEHAVIORS, IF YOU DEVELOP THE HABITS OF SUCCESS, YOU WILL MAKE SUCCESS A HABIT" - LAURA F. POE

TEMPLATES

FITNESS TEST FORM

Name:

Date:

Age:

Weight:

Height:

	TEST	INSTRUCTIONS*	TEST 1	TEST 2	TEST 3
1.	Hexagon				
2.	Medicine Ball Throw				
3.	Spider Drill				
4.	Side Shuffle				
5.	30 feet (10 yard) Dash				
6.	Side to Side				
7.	1.5 Mile Run				
8.	1 Min Push-Ups				
9.	Plank by Time				
10.	1 Min Pull-Ups				

* Look online to find intructions for each fitness test

TECHNIQUE TESTING FORM

Name:	GRIPS					
Age:	FORE	BACK H	VOLLEY F	VOLLEY B	SLICE	SERVE
Dominant Hand:						
Backhand:						
Notes:						

MOVEMENTS				
CLOSE	OPEN	SEMI – OPEN	SLIDE	RECOVERY STEP

STROKES											
PREPARATION				POINT OF CONTACT				FOLLOW THRU			
F	B	V	SL	F	B	V	SL	F	B	V	SL

SERVE								
SLICE			FLAT			SPIN		
PREP	POINT	FOLLOW	PREP	POINT	FOLLOW	PREP	POINT	FOLLOW

CATEGORICAL GOAL PLANNING

	Short Term Goals	Medium Term Goals	Long Term Goals
Name: Date: Age: Dominant Hand:			
Tactical			
Technical			
Physical			
Emotional			
Competitive			

WEEKLY TRAINING CYCLE FORM

CONSISTENCY
MONDAY

SKILL SHOTS
TUESDAY

DEFENSE & OFFENSE
WEDNESDAY

ADAPTATION
THURSDAY

STRATEGY / PLAY
FRIDAY

TOURNAMENT / RECOVERY
SATURDAY

TOURNAMENT / RECOVERY
SUNDAY

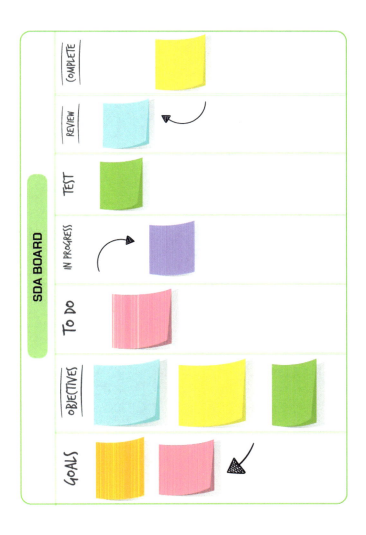

DAILY LESSON PLAN FORM

Monday

Player:
Date:
Coach:
Time Frame:
Objective:
Cycle:

BREAKDOWN	TIME
Warm-up:	
Lesson detail:	
Cool Down:	
Evaluation:	
Self-awareness:	

MATCH/GAME REVIEW FORM

Name: Date:

Dominant Hand:

Opponent Name:

Surface:

Weather Conditions:

QUESTIONS	ANSWERS
What did you do well in today's match/game?	
What could you have done better in today's match/game?	
What did the opponent do well?	
What did the opponent not do well?	
What can I adapt to my process to improve after today's match/game?	

CONCLUSIONS:

BIOGRAPHY OF JHONNATAN MEDINA ALVAREZ

Jhonnatan Medina Alvarez was born on January 12, 1982, in Caracas, Venezuela. At the age of four, he was diagnosed as hyperkinetic, a medical term given to children with a very restless attitude. This made it hard to play group sports, so his parents decided to put him in individual sports. In 1991, when he was 9 years old, a friend of the family, suggested that his parents enroll him in a tennis academy, where he would receive support to carry out his school tasks, and they would give him tennis lessons.

Since that time, his tennis career has given him a lot of satisfaction. He was a champion in all categories in Venezuelan youth tennis. Participated many international tournaments such as the Junior Roland Garros, Wimbledon, US Open, allowing him to make the top 30 in the world as a junior player. During his professional career Jhonnatan was able to reach the top 400 ATP. (Professional ranking). He represented Venezuela in

Davis Cup for 8 years, Pan American, Central American, Bolivarian Games, and managed to be the number one player in his country for singles and doubles.

As the number one player in Venezuela, he was invited to join the staff of tennis commentators on a sports TV channel. An injury to his left hand in 2009 determined his departure from the professional tennis circuit. For that reason, he traveled to the US, underwent surgery, and in 2011, he founded an academy of tennis, *Metro West Tennis Center*, in the city of Orlando, Florida with total success for seven years.

Tennis players rarely say goodbye to tennis, and Jhonnatan decided in 2015 to return to the court again, where he participated in tournaments with another type of mentality, in which playing tennis was more than hitting the ball. It was based on data and decision-making for two years. He managed to win more than 20 tournaments, including the Clay Court National Single Title, and became number one in Florida for Men's 30, and top 10 in the nation.

In 2017, Longwood University opened its doors for him to manage its men's team and later the women's tennis teams as a Director of Tennis and a full-time student. During that time, which he calls "his rebirth", he always shared with his team the importance of leading by example, as he always used the phrase of Albert Einstein: "Setting an example is not the main means of influencing others; it is the only means!"

In May 2021, he graduated from Longwood University in Farmville, Virginia with a Bachelor of Science in Business Administration, *Magna Cum Laude*, with a concentration in Information Systems and Cyber Security. Now since his incursion into the world of pickleball in 2022, Jhonnatan is currently the number one player of his state (Virginia) top 10 in the mid-Atlantic region and top 80 in the world as a single player. Today, Jhonnatan Medina Alvarez presents us his first book, where he writes about his experience as a player, coach, and Scrum Master, coldly exposes his point of view without hesitation on his 30 years on a tennis court, and as Medina says, "My greatest aspiration is that the new generation of players can have this book as a personal guide to understand in detail the importance of the process, culture, and, accountability that are required in the beautiful and unique sports of tennis and pickleball."

Te amo Venezuela

BIOGRAPHY OF LAURA POE

Laura Poe was born in Charleston, WV and spent her early years growing up in the small town of Milton until her family moved to Virginia in 1983, where she remained for nearly 20 years. After graduating from high school, she attended Virginia Commonwealth University and earned two Bachelor of Science degrees in Accounting and Information Systems. She earned her first Master's degree in Information Systems. Shortly after the birth of her second child, she decided to go to seminary and earned a Master's in Theological Studies. In 2019, she completed her terminal studies at Indiana State University, with a Doctor of Philosophy in Technology Management. Some of her research publication subject areas include biometrics, fraud reduction, software quality impacts using rapid delivery methodologies, using Agile as an instructional pedagogy, and leveraging the growth mindset to improve student success.

Her professional background includes ERP supply chain management with 10 years implementing various SAP modules, software development, software testing and quality assurance, cyber security, and Agile coaching. Dr. Poe worked at several large corporations, such as Philip Morris, Dominion Energy, and Capital One, and started her own IT consulting business, DigiTek in 2016. She currently serves as a professor in Information Systems and Cyber Security at Longwood University and was elected to her first term on Colonial Heights City Council in 2020.

At the age of 23, she married her childhood sweetheart, Jason Poe, who she met as a teenager while working at the popular amusement park, Paramount's Kings Dominion. They have two children, Katherine and Joshua. In 2017, she worked with her son on his first fiction book for early readers, *The Crown Jewels of Muddy Creek Mountain*, followed by *The Trouble with Braces*. According to Dr. Poe, "My favorite word is perseverance, and I believe failure is only a perception based upon a pre-determined standard. Having a goal and a plan to get there is the first step towards achieving success. The rest is perseverance and commitment. This book provides a structured plan. You simply need to put the plan into action."

Made in the USA
Thornton, CO
08/02/23 21:24:35

0fc3fae6-fca8-45df-8d7e-00db9e8f6ab7R01